# DAILY RED FLAG JOKES

Colorado Banner

iUniverse, Inc.
Bloomington

# DAILY RED FLAG JOKES

iUniverse books may be ordered through booksellers or by contacting:

iUniverse
1663 Liberty Drive
Bloomington, IN 47403
www.iuniverse.com
1-800-Authors (1-800-288-4677)

Because of the dynamic nature of the Internet, any Web addresses or links contained in this book may have changed since publication and may no longer be valid. The views expressed in this work are solely those of the author and do not necessarily reflect the views of the publisher, and the publisher hereby disclaims any responsibility for them.

Any people depicted in stock imagery provided by Thinkstock are models, and such images are being used for illustrative purposes only.

Certain stock imagery © Thinkstock.

ISBN: 978-1-4502-8251-2 (sc)
ISBN: 978-1-4502-8252-9 (ebk)

Printed in the United States of America

iUniverse rev. date: 12/31/2010

# JANUARY 2011

# SAT. 1

IT MAY BE A RED FLAG
WHEN THE **LIONSHARE**
IN THE COMPANY THAT YOU
HAVE DUMPED AN OBSCENE
AMOUNT OF MONEY INTO
TURNS OUT TO BE NO LARGER
THAN A KITTY CAT.

www.redflagjoke.com

# JANUARY 2011

## SUN. 2

IT MAY BE A RED FLAG WHEN THE TOTAL ATTENDANCE OF YOUR CHURCH HAS DROPPED FROM FIVE HUNDRED TO FIVE, AND THREE OF THEM ARE GOD.

# JANUARY 2011

## MON. 3

IT MAY BE A RED FLAG WHEN
THE MAYOR AND HIS FAMILY
PUSH PAST YOU IN LINE
AT THE HOMELESS SHELTER.

# JANUARY 2011

## TUE. 4

IT MAY BE A RED FLAG WHEN YOUR AMERICAN CHILD IS BEING TAUGHT ENGLISH AS A SECOND LANGUAGE.

# JANUARY 2011

## WED. 5

IT MAY BE A RED FLAG WHEN
YOU GET LESS GAS THAN YOU
WANTED BECAUSE THE PRICE
PER GALLON WENT UP WHILE
YOU WERE WALKING BACK TO
THE PUMP.

# JANUARY 2011

## THU. 6

IT MAY BE A RED FLAG
WHEN YOU ROB FIVE
BANKS AND CALL IT
## "GOING GREEN"

# JANUARY 2011

## FRI. 7

IT MAY BE A RED FLAG
WHEN A WEALTHY MAN
DIES AND LEAVES HIS
CRACKHEAD NEPHEW
A PAWNSHOP.

# JANUARY 2011

## SAT. 8

IT MAY BE A RED FLAG
WHEN PRESIDENT OBAMA
INVITES THE WIZ OF THE KKK
OVER FOR A BEER.

# JANUARY 2011

## SUN. 9

IT MAY BE A RED FLAG WHEN
SISTER LOVEJOY ASKS YOU
TO FIX HER FAUCET AND
MEETS YOU AT THE DOOR
WITH A MARTINI IN EACH
HAND.

# JANUARY 2011

## MON. 10

IT MAY BE A RED FLAG
WHEN YOUR GIRLFRIEND'S
BROTHER'S, UNCLE'S, WIFE'S,
DAD'S, BOSS'S, COLLEGE
BUDDY'S, BESTFRIEND'S,
DAUGHTER'S TWO DAY OLD
TWINS WERE JUST BORN
WHEN I STARTED THIS
SENTENCE.

# JANUARY 2011

## TUE. 11

IT MAY BE A RED FLAG WHEN
A SIXTH GRADE STUDENT IS
OLD ENOUGH
TO VOTE.
[JETHRO BODEEN]

# JANUARY 2011

## WED. 12

IT MAY BE A RED FLAG WHEN
YOUR HOUSE LOOKS BETTER
AFTER THE TORNADO HIT IT.

# JANUARY 2011

## THU. 13

IT MAY BE A RED FLAG WHEN
YOU BUY A VACUUM CLEANER
THAT SAYS IT RECYCLES
DIRT.

# JANUARY 2011

## FRI. 14

IT MAY BE A RED FLAG WHEN
HORSE MANURE IS MARKETED
AS PERSONAL HUMAN
REPELLANT.

# JANUARY 2011

## SAT. 15

IT MAY BE A RED FLAG
WHEN THE DOCTOR AND HIS
STAFF CAN'T STOP LAUGHING
DURING YOUR
PHYSICAL EXAM.

# JANUARY 2011

## SUN. 16

IT MAY BE A RED FLAG WHEN YOUR PASTOR'S CAR IS A $5..................... FOOT LONGER THAN THE CHURCH BUS.

# JANUARY 2011

## MON. 17

IT MAY BE A RED FLAG WHEN
YOUR LAWYER IS FLYING
A SIGN IN FRONT OF THE
COURT HOUSE THAT SAYS
"WILL LIE FOR MONEY"

# JANUARY 2011

## TUE. 18

IT MAY BE A RED FLAG WHEN
YOUR NEW JOB IS REPLACING
A DEAD BULLET PROOF VEST
TESTER.

# JANUARY 2011

## WED. 19

IT MAY BE A RED FLAG
WHEN A GREAT MAN DIES
A VIOLENT DEATH IN THE
U.S WHILE PREACHING AND
TEACHING NONVIOLENCE.

# JANUARY 2011

## THU. 20

IT MAY BE A RED FLAG WHEN
YOU HAVE BEEN COURT
ORDERED TO REGISTER YOUR
MOUTH AS A
LETHAL WEAPON.

# JANUARY 2011

## FRI. 21

IT MAY BE A RED FLAG WHEN
YOUR DOCTOR HAS BEEN
LOOKING FOR YOU FOR TWO
DAYS TO TELL YOU THAT YOU
ONLY HAVE
48 HRS. TO LIVE.

# JANUARY 2011

## SAT. 22

IT MAY BE A RED FLAG WHEN
YOUR FINANCIAL ADVISOR
IS AHEAD OF YOU IN THE
CHECKOUT LINE USING A
FOOD STAMP CARD.

# JANUARY 2011

## SUN. 23

IT MAY BE A RED FLAG WHEN
YOUR CHURCH TAKES UP SO
MANY OFFERINGS THAT YOU
TAKE UP ONE FOR YOURSELF
AND NOBODY NOTICES.

## MON. 24

IT MAY BE A RED FLAG WHEN
YOUR TURN COMES TO PLAY
RUSSIAN ROULETTE, THEY
TOSS YOU AN UZI.

# JANUARY 2011

## TUE. 25

IT MAY BE A RED FLAG WHEN
A POLICEMAN PUTS ON HIS
BULLET PROOF VEST "AFTER"
HE GETS HOME.

# JANUARY 2011

## WED. 26

IT MAY BE A RED FLAG WHEN
THE QUEEN BEE MAKES THE
WORKER BEES LEARN A NEW
WORK SONG ENTITLED
"I GOT MY MIND ON MY
HONEY AND MY HONEY ON
MY MIND"

# JANUARY 2011

## THU. 27

IT MAY BE A RED FLAG WHEN
A BUTCHER SAYS
"IT'S STILL MOVING
CAUSE YOU WANT IT FRESH."

# JANUARY 2011

## FRI. 28

IT MAY BE A RED FLAG
WHEN #1 ON A LIST OF A
MORTICIAN'S
INSTRUCTIONS IS,
"REMOVE ALL SIGNS OF LIFE"

# JANUARY 2011

## SAT. 29

IT MAY BE A RED FLAG WHEN
A CONVENIENCE STORE HAS
A $10 COVER CHARGE.

# JANUARY 2011

## SUN. 30

IT MAY BE A RED FLAG
WHEN JESUS SAYS,
"MY SHEEP WILL WAIT "
"FEED YO KIDS!"

# JANUARY 2011

## MON. 31

IT MAY BE A RED FLAG
WHEN A REALLY ROUGH BAR
INSISTS ON A
"TWO MURDER MINIMUM."

# FEBRUARY 2011

## TUE. 1

IT MAY BE A RED FLAG WHEN
THE INTERNATIONAL HOUSE
OF PANCAKES GANGSTAS
HAS A MOTTO OF
"SYRUP IN AND BUTTER OUT"

# FEBRUARY 2011

## WED. 2

IT MAY BE A RED FLAG WHEN
YOUR NEIGHBOR THAT'S
ALWAYS FIGHTING WITH
HIS WIFE ASKS IF HE CAN
BORROW A CUP OF POISON.

# FEBRUARY 2011

## THU. 3

IT MAY BE A RED FLAG
WHEN THE PEOPLE AT
YOUR FUNERAL ARE NOT
CONCERNED ABOUT WHERE
YOU WENT, THEY'RE JUST
GLAD YOU DID.

# FEBRUARY 2011

## FRI. 4

IT MAY BE A RED FLAG WHEN
THEY CHANGE THE NAME OF
THE DOLLAR STORE TO
"THE DOLLAR STORE YEAH RIGHT"

# FEBRUARY 2011

## SAT. 5

IT MAY BE A RED FLAG WHEN YOU TAKE YOUR BABY INTO A RESTROOM MARKED "FAMILY" AND FIND A GUY, HIS WIFE, AND MOTHER-IN-LAW PLAYING MONOPLY.

# FEBRUARY 2011

## SUN. 6

IT MAY BE A RED FLAG WHEN "I PITY THE FOOL BAPTIST CHURCH" MEMBERS DON'T WANT TO GO TO HEAVEN BECAUSE THEY'RE ALL AFRAID TO FLY.

# FEBRUARY 2011

## MON. 7

IT MAY BE A RED FLAG WHEN A SIGN IN A RESTAURANT RESTROOM SAYS "OPTIONAL WASHING OF HANDS BY EMPLOYEES IS MANDATORY."

# FEBRUARY 2011

## TUE. 8

IT MAY BE A RED FLAG WHEN
A POLICE DEPARTMENT'S
RESPONSE TO A CRIME IN
PROGRESS IS TIMED ON A
CALENDAR.

# FEBRUARY 2011

## WED. 9

IT MAY BE A RED FLAG WHEN
THE CUSTOMERS YOU SERVE
THINK THAT "TIP" IS THE
WAY THEY SHOULD WALK
WHEN LEAVING YOUR TABLE
WITHOUT ONE.

# FEBRUARY 2011

## THU. 10

IT MAY BE A RED FLAG WHEN
A BANK TELLER HAS NOT
RETURNED AFTER 3 DAYS
FROM A ONE HR.LUNCH.

# FEBRUARY 2011

## FRI. 11

IT MAY BE A RED FLAG WHEN
THE DRIVER IN YOUR CAR
POOL PULLS UP TO A TRAFFIC
LIGHT AND ASK YOU WHAT
COLOR IT IS.

# FEBRUARY 2011

## SAT. 12

IT MAY BE A RED FLAG WHEN
THE RAISINS IN YOUR
OATMEAL WEREN'T THERE A
MINUTE AGO.

# FEBRUARY 2011

## SUN. 13

IT MAY BE A RED FLAG WHEN YOUR PASTOR'S DIAMOND RING IS SO BIG THAT THE USHER GIVES YOU A PAIR OF DARK GLASSES AND A SEEING EYE DOG AT THE DOOR.

# FEBRUARY 2011

## MON. 14

IT MAY BE A RED FLAG
WHEN A MAN PLEADS NOT
GUILTY TO A CHARGE OF
INDECENT EXPOSURE FOR
MOONING THE POPE BECAUSE
HE SAYS IT WAS A
"WARDROBE MALFUNCTION."

# FEBRUARY 2011

## TUE. 15

IT MAY BE A RED FLAG
WHEN AS A RESULT OF THE
DECISION BY THE U.S. TO
IMPORT CHICKENS FROM
MEXICO, THE REPUBLICAN
PARTY IS CONSIDERING
USING AS THEIR NEXT
PRESIDENTIAL CAMPAIGN
SLOGAN,
"SOME POT IN EVERY
CHICKEN."

# FEBRUARY 2011

## WED. 16

IT MAY BE A RED FLAG WHEN
YOU HEAR A TRAIN RIGHT
OUTSIDE YOUR HOUSE AND
THERE'S NO TRACK FOR
MILES.

# FEBRUARY 2011

## THU. 17

IT MAY BE A RED FLAG
WHEN INSTEAD OF LICENSE,
REGISTRATION AND PROOF
OF INSURANCE, THE STATE
TROOPER ASKS YOU FOR
DINNER AND A MOVIE.

# FEBRUARY 2011

## FRI. 18

IT MAY BE A RED FLAG
WHEN YOUR GENUINE GOLD
BRACELET TURNS THE WHOLE
LEFT SIDE OF YOUR
BODY GREEN.

# FEBRUARY 2011

## SAT. 19

IT MAY BE A RED FLAG
WHEN THE FAMILY OF DUST
BUNNIES UNDER YOUR BED
GO BACK 3 GENERATIONS.

# FEBRUARY 2011

## SUN. 20

IT MAY BE A RED FLAG WHEN
THE YOUNGEST MEMBER OF
YOUR CHURCH'S YOUTH GROUP
IS ON A PENSION.

# FEBBUARY 2011

## MON. 21

IT MAY BE A RED FLAG WHEN
YOU CAN'T UNDERSTAND WHY
YOU FAILED A DRUG TEST
THAT YOU STAYED UP ALL
NIGHT STUDYING FOR.

# FEBRUARY 2011

## TUE. 22

IT MAY BE A RED FLAG WHEN
YOUR FEET ARE SO ROUGH
THAT THEY STRIKE SPARKS
ON ASPHALT THAT CAN BE
SEEN FROM SPACE.

# FEBRUARY 2011

## WED. 23

IT MAY BE A RED FLAG WHEN
A BOXER IS SO CROSSEYED
THAT HE KNOCKED OUT SOME
DUDE IN THE THIRD ROW.

# FEBRUARY 2011

## THU. 24

IT MAY BE A RED FLAG WHEN
YOUR CRACKHEAD BROTHER
STEALS THE CD PLAYER OUT
OF YOUR CAR AT YALL'S
MAMA'S FUNERAL.

# FEBRUARY 2011

## FRI. 25

IT MAY BE A RED FLAG WHEN A POLICEMAN TESTS HIS STATE OF THE ART VERBAL BREATHALYZER AND IT SAYS, "YOU HAVE THE RIGHT TO REMAIN SILENT."

# FEBRUARY 2011

## SAT. 26

IT MAY BE A RED FLAG
WHEN YOU AVOID BRIDGES
WITH LOAD LIMITS
WHEN YOUR MOTHER-IN-
LAW IS IN THE CAR.

# FEBRUARY 2011

## SUN 27

IT MAY BE A RED FLAG WHEN THE NAME OF YOUR CHURCH IS CHANGED FROM "MT. HOPE" TO "MT. DOPE."

# FEBRUARY 2011

## MON. 28

IT MAY BE A RED FLAG WHEN A STREET SWEEPER DRIVER DUMPS AT THE END OF EVERY BLOCK SO HIS CRACKHEAD BUDDIES CAN SIFT THE DIRT FOR CHANGE.

# MARCH 2011

## TUE. 1

IT MAY BE A RED FLAG WHEN YOU GET YOUR PROCTOLOGIST AND YOUR PODIATRIST CONFUSED WITH EACH OTHER.

# MARCH 2011

## WED. 2

IT MAY BE A RED FLAG WHEN
A THREE LEGGED HORSE IS
THE ODDS ON FAVORITE IN
THE KENTUCKY DERBY.

# MARCH 2011

## THU. 3

IT MAY BE A RED FLAG WHEN
A GANG MEMBER OF "THE
BLOODS" IS COLOR BLIND
AND MISTAKENLY DRESSES
IN BLUE.

# MARCH 2011

## FRI. 4

IT MAY BE A RED FLAG
WHEN A HALON FACTORY,
THE WATER DEPARTMENT,
AND A FIRE EXTINGUISHER
ASSEMBLY PLANT ALL BURN
DOWN ON THE SAME DAY.

# MARCH 2011

## SAT. 5

IT MAY BE A RED FLAG
WHEN YOUR FLIGHT HAS
BEEN DIVERTED FROM
POUGHKEEPSIE TO PARIS
WITH THE CAPTAIN AND HIS
CREW DRESSED IN ORANGE
JUMPSUITS.

# MARCH 2011

## SUN. 6

IT MAY BE A RED FLAG WHEN
THE NAME OF YOUR CHURCH
HAS BEEN CHANGED FROM
"FIRST METHODIST," TO
"FIRST METHADONE."

# MARCH 2011

## MON. 7

IT MAY BE A RED FLAG
WHEN YOU RUSH YOUR PET
ROCK TO THE EMERGENCY
ROOM BECAUSE IT'S NOT
BREATHING.

# MARCH 2011

## TUE. 8

IT MAY BE A RED FLAG WHEN
YOU GET TOO OLD TO DIE SO
THE "UGLY POLICE" COME AND
TAKE YOU AWAY.

# MARCH 2011

## WED. 9

IT MAY BE A RED FLAG
WHEN A WOMAN'S CLOTHES
ARE SO TIGHT THAT YOU
FLINCH EVERY TIME SHE
MOVES FROM FEAR OF AN
EXPLOSION.

# MARCH 2011

## THU. 10

IT MAY BE A RED FLAG WHEN
YOUR WIFE PUTS YOU ON
"AMERICA'S 10 MOST
UNWANTED" LIST.

# MARCH 2011

## FRI. 11

IT MAY BE A RED FLAG
WHEN YOU ARE SO SHORT
YOU HAVE TO STAND ON
A LADDER TO HIGH FIVE
EMMANUEL LEWIS.

# MARCH 2011

## SAT. 12

IT MAY BE A RED FLAG WHEN
YOU CONTINUE TO SUPPRESS
YOUR CHILD'S CREATIVITY
EVEN THOUGH GOD MADE HIM
SMARTER THAN YOU.

# MARCH 2011

## SUN. 13

IT MAY BE A RED FLAG WHEN
YOUR LIFE IS SO MESSED UP
THAT JESUS GIVES YOU A
REFERRAL.

# MARCH 2011

## MON. 14

IT MAY BE A RED FLAG WHEN
YOU THINK MOUNTAIN
OYSTERS COME FROM HIGH
ALTITUDE LAKES.

# MARCH 2011

## TUE. 15

IT MAY BE A RED FLAG WHEN
YOU THINK FASTING IS THE
OPPOSITE OF SLOWING.

# MARCH 2011

## WED. 16

IT MAY BE A RED FLAG
WHEN IMMEDIATELY AFTER
HEARING YOUR CONFESSION
THE PRIEST JOINS THE
WITNESS RELOCATION
PRROGRAM.

# MARCH 2011

## THU. 17

IT MAY BE A RED FLAG WHEN
YOUR TIRES ARE SO THIN
YOU CAN SEE THE FIX-A-
FLAT INSIDE.

# MARCH 2011

## FRI. 18

IT MAY BE A RED FLAG WHEN
YOU ARE ASK TO LEAVE THE
BANK FOR WEARING A MASK,
BUT AREN'T.

# MARCH 2011

## SAT. 19

IT MAY BE A RED FLAG WHEN
YOU GO TO A MASQUERADE
PARTY DISGUISED AS YOUR
IDENTICAL TWIN.

# MARCH 2011

## SUN. 20

IT MAY BE A RED FLAG WHEN
YOUR PASTOR SAYS HE
GONNA CLOSE, BUT NEVER
DOES.

# MARCH 2011

## MON. 21

IT MAY BE A RED FLAG WHEN
ELVIS PRESLEY AND MICHAEL
JACKSON ARE SPOTTED AT
A KISS CONCERT WITH RAY
CHARLES AND GARY COLEMAN.

# MARCH 2011

## TUE. 22

IT MAY BE A RED FLAG WHEN
SOMEONE POPS YOU IN THE
EYE AND TELLS YOU HOW
GOOD IT'S GONNA FEEL
WHEN IT STOPS HURTING.

# MARCH 2011

## WED. 23

IT MAY BE A RED FLAG WHEN
YOU *GO* TO HELL AND DON'T
SEE NOBODY YOU KNOW.

# MARCH 2011

## THU. 24

IT MAY BE A RED FLAG
WHEN YOU BREAK TWO
COMMANDMENTS AT THE
SAME TIME, BY
## KILLING
me with yo
## LIES.

# MARCH 2011

## FRI. 25

IT MAY BE A RED FLAG WHEN
ROACHES ARE HAVING A
MILLION MAN MARCH IN THE
SCHOOL CAFETERIA.

# MARCH 2011

## SAT. 26

IT MAY BE A RED FLAG WHEN
YOU SEE A DEER IN AN
ORANGE CAP, DRESSED IN
CAMO AND DRIVING A JEEP
WITH A MAN STRAPPED TO
THE HOOD.

# MARCH 2011

## SUN. 27

IT MAY BE A RED FLAG WHEN YOU WALK INTO CHURCH WITH YOUR FAVORITE RED AND WHITE OUTFIT ON, THEY HAND YOU A BLUE PROGRAM, AND EVERYBOBY STANDS UP AND SALUTES.

# MARCH 2011

## MON. 28

IT MAY BE A RED FLAG WHEN
YOUR FITNESS INSTRUCTOR
IS SO FAT THAT A DOUBLE
MEAT WHOPPER LOOKS LIKE A
NICKEL IN HIS HAND.

# MARCH 2011

## TUE. 29

IT MAY BE A RED FLAG WHEN
YOUR DENTIST'S TEETH LOOK
LIKE A MINIATURE REPLICA
OF STONEHENGE.

# MARCH 2011

## WED. 30

IT MAY BE A RED FLAG WHEN
IN RESPONSE TO YOUR
GOOD MORNING THE WAL
MART GREETER SAYS, "YEAH
RIGHT."

# MARCH 2011

## THU. 31

IT MAY BE A RED FLAG WHEN
YOUR MARRIAGE COUNSELOR
INTRODUCES YOU TO TWO OF
HIS WIVES.

# APRIL 2011

## FRI. 1

IT MAY BE A RED FLAG WHEN
THE PCH PRIZE PATROL
DRIVES UP, KNOCKS ON YOUR
DOOR, YELLS,
**"APRIL FOOL!"**
AND DRIVES OFF.

# APRIL 2011

## SAT. 2

IT MAY BE A RED FLAG
WHEN THE CEMENT IN YOUR
DRIVEWAY IS SO THIN THAT
THE POTATO CHIP FACTORY
WANTS TO KNOW
YOUR SECRET.

# APRIL 2011

## SUN. 3

IT MAY BE A RED FLAG
WHEN YOU DISCOVER
THAT DONKEY'S CAN
TALK 'WITHOUT' GOD'S
EMPOWERMENT.

# APRIL 2011

## MON. 4

IT MAY BE A RED FLAG WHEN
MY BROTHER RONNIE RIDES
A BAD TO THE BONE STREET
GLIDE HARLEY WITH
TRAINING WHEELS.

# APRIL 2011

## TUE. 5

IT MAY BE A RED FLAG WHEN THE LADY IN THE WHITE UNIFORM REFUSES TO SIGN YOU UP FOR YOUR MILITARY BENEFITS AT THE VETERINARIAN'S OFFICE.

# APRIL 2011

## WED. 6

IT MAY BE A RED FLAG
WHEN YOU SEE A U-HAUL
TRUCK LEADING A FUNERAL
PROCESSION.

# APRIL 2011

## THU. 7

IT MAY BE A RED FLAG WHEN
YOU SAVE ALL YOUR BURNED
OUT LIGHT BULBS TO BUILD A
DARKROOM.

# APRIL 2011

## FRI. 8

IT MAY BE A RED FLAG WHEN YOUR C.P.A. COUNTS ON HIS FINGERS AND USES A FAT PENCIL.

# APRIL 2011

## SAT. 9

IT MAY BE A RED FLAG WHEN
A MAN AND HIS WIFE ARE
ASKED TO LEAVE THEIR
WHEELBARROW AND SHOVEL
OUTSIDE AN ALL YOU CAN
EAT BUFFET.

# APRIL 2011

## SUN. 10

IT MAY BE A RED FLAG WHEN
THE GUY THAT PORTRAYED
JESUS IN THE EASTER PLAY
HOSTED A CHURCH YARD SALE
AND RAN OFF WITH ALL
THE MONEY.

# APRIL 2011

## MON. 11

IT MAY BE A RED FLAG WHEN
YOUR PROMISCUOUS BOSS
TAKES YOU TO AN
"ALL YOU CAN CHEAT
BUFFET."

# APRIL 2011

## TUE. 12

IT MAY BE A RED FLAG WHEN THE SPACE SHUTTLE CREW DISCOVERS AN UNHAPPY COLONY OF AFRICANIZED HONEY BEES ON BOARD.

# APRIL 2011

## WED. 13

IT MAY BE A RED FLAG WHEN
CHURCH MEMBERS ACT LIKE
THEY DON'T RECOGNIZE YOU
IN THE LIQUOR STORE.

# APRIL 2011

## THU. 14

IT MAY BE A RED FLAG WHEN
MARTHA STEWART BUYS WAL
MART OUT AND RENAMES IT
"WAL MARTHA"

# APRIL 2011

## FRI. 15

IT MAY BE A RED FLAG WHEN
A GUY SHOWS YOU HIS ELVIS
IMPRESSION BY SPOUTING
RACIAL SLURS AND STICKING
A NEEDLE IN HIS ARM.

# APRIL 2011

## SAT. 16

IT MAY BE A RED FLAG WHEN THE BUM AT THE INTERSECTION ADJACENT TO THE LARGEST LIQUOR STORE IN TOWN IS FLYING A SIGN THAT SAYS "WILL DRINK WITH YOUR MONEY."

# APRIL 2011

## SUN. 17

IT MAY BE A RED FLAG
WHEN ONE OF YOUR CHURCH
MEMBERS LEAVES TOWN AS
BILLY JOHN JACKSON AND
COMES BACK AS BILLIE JEAN
JACKED UP.

# APRIL 2011

## MON. 18

IT MAY BE A RED FLAG
WHEN YOUR GOSSIPY AUNT'S
BUSINESS CARD SAYS, "HAVE
LIE WILL TRAVEL."

# APRIL 2011

## TUE. 19

IT MAY BE A RED FLAG WHEN YOUR WIG MAKES ITS WAY HOME AFTER BEING BLOWN OFF IN ANOTHER TOWN, IN ANOTHER STATE.

# APRIL 2011

## WED. 20

# IT MAY BE A RED FLAG WHEN A TATTOO PARLOR HAS A SIGN THAT SAYS "FREE BODY PIERCING"

ON VITAL ORGANS ONLY

# APRIL 2011

## THU. 21

IT MAY BE A RED FLAG WHEN
ON THE 18TH MILE OF THE
NYC MARATHON YOU OBSERVE
ONE OF THE CONTESTANTS
EMERGING FROM A TAXI.

# APRIL 2011

## FRI. 22

IT MAY BE A RED FLAG WHEN
YOUR LEASE CONTRACT
STATES IN THE FINE PRINT
THAT THE RATS IN THE
BASEMENT HAVE A SUB.

# APRIL 2011

## SAT. 23

IT MAY BE A RED FLAG WHEN
YOUR COOK STOVE IS SO
OLD THAT WHEN IT QUITS
WORKING, IT'S OUT OF
WOOD.

# APRIL 2011

## SUN. 24

IT MAY BE A RED FLAG WHEN THE 400 LB. CHURCH FOOD BANK DIRECTOR CLOSES UP AND HANGS A SIGN ON THE DOOR THAT SAYS "THINK FAST."

# APRIL 2011

## MON. 25

IT MAY BE A RED FLAG
WHEN YOUR BABY'S EARS
ARE BLOCKING YOUR LINE OF
SIGHT IN BOTH REAR VIEW
MIRRORS.

# APRIL 2011

## TUE. 26

IT MAY BE A RED FLAG WHEN
YOU THINK CATATONIC IS
AN ELIXER FOR FELINES.

# APRIL 2011

## WED. 27

IT MAY BE A RED FLAG WHEN
A WASHED UP POLICE DOG
HOLDS A SIGN THAT SAYS,
"WILL SNIFF FOR FOOD."

# APRIL 2011

## THU. 28

IT MAY BE A RED FLAG WHEN
A COMPANY DOWNSIZES
ITS PAYROLL BY REPLACING
YOU WITH AN ILLEGAL
IMMIGRANT.............. MONKEY.

# APRIL 2011

## FRI. 29

IT MAY BE A RED FLAG WHEN
YOU THINK "DRINK" AND
"RESPONSIBLY" BELONG IN
THE SAME SENTENCE.

# APRIL 2011

## SAT. 30

IT MAY BE A RED FLAG WHEN
A GIRL WITH A BODY LIKE
A REFRIGERATOR MAGNET
AUDITIONS FOR A SUPER
MODEL JOB.

# MAY 2011

## SUN. 1

IT MAY BE A RED FLAG WHEN
JESUS SAYS,
"YOU HAVE NOT BECAUSE
YOU ASK NOT"
.................FOR A JOB.

# MAY 2011

## MON. 2

IT MAY BE A RED FLAG
WHEN A PANTY HOSE
SPOKES MODEL'S KNEES
LOOK LIKE A GUNNY SACK
FULL OF GOLF BALLS.

# MAY 2011

## TUE. 3

IT MAY BE A RED FLAG WHEN
YOU THINK A HOSPICE IS A
HOTEL RUN BY A BUNCH OF
OVER THE HILL
"SPICE GIRLS."

# MAY 2011

## WED. 4

IT MAY BE A RED FLAG WHEN
THE FOOD IS SO BAD THAT
YOU TELL THE WAITRESS YOU
WANT YOUR ORDER TO GO,
BUT YOU'RE STAYING.

# MAY 2011

## THU. 5

IT MAY BE A RED FLAG WHEN
A SIGN IN A SANDWICH
SHOP SAYS, "PLEASE EXCUSE
OUR ROACHES, THEY
PROMISED TO BE OUT BY THE
END OF THE MONTH."

# MAY 2011

## FRI. 6

IT MAY BE A RED FLAG WHEN
A SIGN IN A DRUG STORE
READS; ALL WEIGHT LOSS
PLANS AND DIET AIDS, ARE
HEREBY DISCONTINUED;
SINCE
AIN'T NOBODY LOSING
NO WEIGHT NO HOW.

# MAY 2011

## SAT. 7

IT MAY BE A RED FLAG WHEN
A FUNERAL PARLOR RUNS
AN AD THAT SAYS, "WE ARE
NOW ACCEPTING BODIES
WITHOUT
EXPIRATION DATES."

# MAY 2011

## SUN. 8

IT MAY BE A RED FLAG WHEN YOUR PASTORS KIDS ARE SO BAD THAT HE HAS A POLICE SUBSTATION IN HIS LIVNG ROOM.

# MAY 2011

## MON. 9

IT MAY BE A RED FLAG
WHEN A WITCH DOCTOR
SHRINKS STEVE HARVEY'S
HEAD SO THAT HE CAN
WEAR A SIZE 9 HAT.

# MAY 2011

## TUE. 10

IT MAY BE A RED FLAG
WHEN NOBODY RESPECTS
YOU EXCEPT PEOPLE THAT
NOBODY RESPECT.

# MAY 2011

# WED. 11

IT MAY BE A RED FLAG
WHEN A DOCTOR GIVES
HIS REALLY OLD PATIENT'S
CALENDARS WITH HALF
THE PAGES TORN OFF.

# MAY 2011

## THU. 12

IT MAY BE A RED FLAG
WHEN YOU THINK AN
ELLIPTICAL TRAINER IS AN
INSTRUCTION BOOKLET ON
THE CORRECT WAY TO LOOK
AT THE SUN WHEN IT GOES
BEHIND THE MOON.

# MAY 2011

## FRI. 13

IT MAY BE A RED FLAG WHEN
YOU STAY INSIDE ON THIS
DAY BECAUSE YOU THINK
YOUR LUCK IS GONNA STINK
WORSE THAN ALL YOUR
OTHER STINKY DAYS.

# MAY 2011

## SAT. 14

IT MAY BE A RED FLAG
WHEN YOUR WHOLE
FAMILY HAS BEEN HIRED
TO STAND OUTSIDE THE
DOCTOR'S OFFICE TO
MAKE PEOPLE SICK.

# MAY 2011

## SUN. 15

IT MAY BE A RED FLAG
WHEN YOUR PASTOR SHAKES
HANDS WITH A WOMAN AT
THE END OF THE SERVICE
AND IS STILL HOLDING ON
WHEN SHE PULLS INTO HER
DRIVEWAY.

# MAY 2011

## MON. 16

IT MAY BE A RED FLAG WHEN
YOU HAVE REFINANCED YOUR
HOUSE SO MANY TIMES THAT
YOUR PAYOFF DATE IS THE
15TH OF NEVAUARY.

# MAY 2011

# TUE. 17

IT MAY BE A RED FLAG
WHEN THE DEPT FOR THE
PREVENTION OF THE SPREAD
OF S.T.D.s ASKS YOU TO
POSE FOR THEIR CALENDAR.

# MAY 2011

## WED. 18

IT MAY BE A RED FLAG
WHEN YOUR GIRLFRIEND'S
PARENTS DRESS YOU IN
A BIO SUIT BEFORE YOU
CAN ENTER HER ROOM.

# MAY 2011

## THU. 19

IT MAY BE A RED FLAG WHEN
YOUR HYGIENE IS SO BAD
THAT YOUR SHOWER JOINED
THE WITNESS RELOCATION
PROGRAM.

# MAY 2011

## FRI. 20

IT MAY BE A RED FLAG
WHEN YOUR FIREWALKER
INSTRUCTOR SHOWS UP
WEARING
ASBESTOS BOOTS.

# MAY 2011

## SAT. 21

IT MAY BE A RED FLAG WHEN
AN AD READS "WANTED,
PEOPLE WITH LARGE HEADS
TO HELP TEST THE EFFECTS
OF BLUNT FORCE TRAUMA."

# MAY 2011

## SUN. 22

IT MAY BE A RED FLAG WHEN
YOUR PASTOR FALLS SLEEP
IN THE MIDDLE OF HIS OWN
SERMON.

# MAY 2011

## MON. 23

IT MAY BE A RED FLAG WHEN
A SPEECH BEGINS WITH,
"THIS IS GONNA HURT ME
WORSE THAN IT'S GONNA
HURT YOU."

# MAY 2011

## TUE. 24

IT MAY BE A RED FLAG WHEN
THE DIRTY CAR POLICE PULL
YOU OVER WITH PRESSURE
WASHERS DRAWN.

# MAY 2011

## WED. 25

IT MAY BE A RED FLAG WHEN
YOUR GRASS IS SO TALL
THAT ALL YOU CAN SEE OUT
YOUR WINDOW IS A BEAR
NURSING HER CUBS ON YOUR
FRONT PORCH.

# MAY 2011

## THU. 26

IT MAY BE A RED FLAG
WHEN A PERSON'S FIRST
STATEMENT IS, "BUT I
DIDN'T KNOW IT
WAS LOADED."

# MAY 2011

## FRI. 27

IT MAY BE A RED FLAG WHEN
YOUR NEED TO PLEASE IS
OUT WEIGHED BY YOUR NEED
TO DO THE RIGHT THING.

# MAY 2011

## SAT. 28

IT MAY BE A RED FLAG WHEN O.J. IS MAD BECAUSE HE DIDN'T WIN THE #1 SPOT ON "AMERICA'S STUPIDEST CRIMINALS."

[FOR MY MONEY HE DID]

# MAY 2011

## SUN. 29

IT MAY BE A RED FLAG WHEN
THERE IS SO MUCH GUM ON
THE CARPET OF YOUR CHURCH
THAT THEY PASS OUT PUTTY
KNIVES AT THE ALTER.

# MAY 2011

## MON. 30

IT MAY BE A RED FLAG WHEN
YOU WASH YOUR FEET WITH
YOUR SOX ON.

# MAY 2011

## TUE. 31

IT MAY BE A RED FLAG WHEN
SATAN SENDS YOU AN
INVITATION MARKED
"R.S.V.P."

# JUNE 2011

# WED. 1

IT MAY BE A RED FLAG
WHEN YOU KNOW THAT
CRACK IS THE SINGLE MOST
ADDICTIVE, PERVERSE,
DEMON POSSESSED,
SOUL KILLING, FAMILY
DESTROYING, RED EYE
EXPRESS VEHICLE TO HELL
DRUG ON THIS PLANET.
AND YOU STILL
PUFFING.

www.redflagjoke.com

# JUN 2011

## THU. 2

IT MAY BE A RED FLAG
WHEN YOU CHANGE YOUR
UNDERWEAR LESS THAN YOU
DO YOUR OIL.

# JUNE 2011

## FRI. 3

IT MAY BE A RED FLAG WHEN
THE UGLY POLICE PULL YOU
OVER AND STUFF PRO BONO
PLASTIC SURGEON'S PHONE
NUMBERS IN YOUR
SHIRT POCKET.

# JUNE 2011

# SAT. 4

IT MAY BE A RED FLAG WHEN
YOUR MECHANIC GIVES YOU
HIS BILL ALONG WITH A BOX
FULL OF LEFT OVER BOLTS.

# JUNE 2011

## SUN. 5

IT MAY BE A RED FLAG WHEN YOUR CHURCH PUTS ADVANCE PAYDAY LOAN APPLICATIONS INSIDE THEIR OFFERING ENVELOPES.

# JUNE 2011

## MON. 6

IT MAY BE A RED FLAG WHEN
YOU BUILD YOUR HOUSE
WITH A BLUEPRINT THAT
YOU BORROWED FROM # 1 OF
THE THREE LITTLE PIGS.

# JUNE 2011

## TUE. 7

IT MAY BE A RED FLAG WHEN
GETTING CAR INSURANCE
TURNS OUT TO BE A WAY
TOO COMPLICATED FOR THE
CAVEMAN.

# JUNE 2011

## WED. 8

IT MAY BE A RED FLAG
WHEN YOU HEAP COALS
INTO YOUR BOSOM AND
ARE SHOCKED WHEN YOUR
SHIRT CATCHES FIRE.

# JUNE 2011

## THU. 9

IT MAY BE A RED FLAG
WHEN THE FREEWAY
HAS MORE HUMPS AND
BUMPS THAN A GANG OF
PREPUBESCENT TEENAGERS
IN A CAMEL RACE.

# JUNE 2011

## FRI. 10

IT MAY BE A RED FLAG WHEN
THERE ARE FEATHERS STUCK
ALL OVER YOUR SNORING
WIFE'S FACE AND HER BIRD
CAGE IS EMPTY.

# JUNE 2011

## SAT. 11

IT MAY BE A RED FLAG WHEN
"HENCO EN MEXICO"
IS STAMPED ON THE BOTTOM
Of YOUR ITALIAN LOAFERS.

# JUNE 2011

## SUN. 12

IT MAY BE A RED FLAG WHEN
YOU PUT A DOLLAR IN THE
OFFERING PLATE AND TAKE
OUT CHANGE FOR A TWENTY.

# JUNE 2011

## MON. 13

IT MAY BE A RED FLAG WHEN YOUR HOUSE IS SO OLD THAT THE MUD BETWEEN THE LOGS NEEDS REPLACING.

# JUNE 2011

## TUE. 14

IT MAY BE A RED
FLAG WHEN RONALD
MCDONALD IS REPLACED
BY KRUSTY THE KLOWN.

# JUNE 2011

## WED. 15

IT MAY BE A RED FLAG WHEN ITCHY AND SCRATCHY OPEN A DOMESTIC VIOLENCE COUNSELING CENTER WITH BOBBY BROWN, IKE TURNER, SUSAN SMITH, CHRIS BROWN, ROBERT BLAKE, AND O.J. SIMPSON ON THE BOARD OF DIRECTORS.

# JUNE 2011

## THU. 16

IT MAY BE A RED FLAG WHEN
A DOG IS SO MALNOURISHED
THAT HE HAS TO GET THE
NEIGHBOR DOG TO COME
OVER TO BARK FOR HIM.

# JUNE 2011

## FRI. 17

IT MAY BE A RED FLAG WHEN
THE ROACHES NEXT DOOR
JACK THE DELIVERY BOY FOR
YOUR PIZZA.

# JUNE 2011

## SAT. 18

IT MAY BE A RED FLAG WHEN
THE STATUE OF LIBERTY
TRADES HER TORCH IN FOR A
FLAME THROWER.

# JUNE 2011

# SUN. 19

IT MAY BE A RED FLAG
WHEN TWO STRANGERS
ARE SEEN EXITING THE
REAR OF THE CHURCH WITH
THE OFFERING BUCKETS.

# JUNE 2011

## MON. 20

IT MAY BE A RED FLAG WHEN
THE STATE OF CALIFORNIA
GOT SO BROKE THAT THE
GOVERNOR TRIED TO PAWN
HIS ACCENT.

# JUNE 2011

## TUE. 21

IT MAY BE A RED FLAG
WHEN YOU TAKE YOUR
MOTHER OUT TO DINNER
AND ASK THE WAITER
FOR SEPARATE CHECKS.

# JUNE 2011

## WED. 22

IT MAY BE A RED FLAG
WHEN YOUR BLIND GRANDMA
SPENDS ONLY HALF THE TIME
CLEANING CHITTLINS AS
EVERYBODY ELSE.

# JUNE 2011

## THU. 23

IT MAY BE A RED FLAG
WHEN THE "BOTTOM OF THE
BARREL" DATING SERVICE
HOOKS YOU UP WITH YOUR
EX-WIFE'S, EX-HUSBAND'S,
EX-WIFE.

# JUNE 2011

## FRI. 24

IT MAY BE A RED FLAG WHEN
IF THERE'S NO "I" IN TEAM
AND NO "U" IN TEAM, COACH
MUS AIN'T GONNA
LET US PLAY.

# JUNE 2011

## SAT. 25

IT MAY BE A RED FLAG WHEN
YOU GIVE A "GIFT HORSE" A
TONSILECTOMY.

# JUNE 2011

## SUN. 26

IT MAY BE A RED FLAG WHEN
SOME PEOPLE BELIEVE THAT
JESUS CAME TO NORTH
AMERICA IN THE 1900s,
WROTE A NEW BIBLE AND
WAS A WHITE MAN.

# JUNE 2011

# MON. 27

IT MAY BE A RED FLAG WHEN YOUR HOUSE IS COMPLETELY DESTROYED IN A 1.0 EARTHQUAKE.

# JUNE 2011

## TUE. 28

IT MAY BE A RED FLAG WHEN
YOUR DOCTER TELLS YOU
TO USE THE SCALES AT THE
TRUCKSTOP AND BRING THE
WEIGHT TICKET TO YOUR
PHYSICAL EXAM.

# JUNE 2011

## WED. 29

IT MAY BE A RED FLAG
WHEN AFTER YOU'VE BEEN
ARRESTED, HANDCUFFED, AND
PLACED IN THE BACK SEAT,
THE SQUAD CAR HEADS IN
THE OPPOSITE DIRECTION OF
THE POLICE STATION.

# JUNE 2011

## THU. 30

IT MAY BE A RED FLAG
WHEN YOUR BARBER
SHAVES AND TEXTS YOU
AT THE SAME TIME.

# JULY 2011

## FRI. 1

IT MAY BE A RED FLAG WHEN
THE AMERICAN MALE BITES
THE DUST AN AVERAGE OF 2
1/2 YRS. AFTER HE RETIRES.

# JULY 2011

## SAT. 2

IT MAY BE A RED FLAG WHEN
MOST PEOPLE DON'T KNOW
THAT AN ANTIQUATED
DEFINITION FOR "RETIRE" IS
"TO DIE........"

# JULY 2011

## SUN. 3

IT MAY BE A RED FLAG WHEN
YOU LEAVE JESUS IN PRISON
WHERE YOU FOUND HIM AND
DON'T HOLLA FOR HIM AGAIN
UNTIL YOU GO BACK.

# JULY 2011

## MON. 4

IT MAY BE A RED FLAG
WHEN THE WEEDS IN
YOUR BACKYARD ARE SO
TALL THAT SASQUATCH
HAS LIVED THERE
UNDETECTED FOR YEARS.

# JULY 2011

## TUE. 5

IT MAY BE A RED FLAG
WHEN YOU NEARLY STARVE
TO DEATH EVERY TIME
SOMEBODY HIDES YOUR FOOD
STAMP CARD UNDER YOUR
WORK BOOTS.

# JULY 2011

## WED. 6

IT MAY BE A RED FLAG WHEN
YOU ARE SO RICH THAT YOU
THINK THAT HEAVEN WOULD
BE SLUMMING.

# JULY 2011

## THU. 7

IT MAY BE A RED FLAG WHEN THE RECEPTIONIST AT A CHEESE FACTORY BEARS AN UNCANNY RESEMBLANCE TO A GIANT RAT.

# JULY 2011

## FRI. 8

IT MAY BE A RED FLAG WHEN
YOU FIND GUNS, DRUGS, AND
PORNO UNDER YOUR 82 YR.
OLD SON'S MATTRESS.

# JULY 2011

## SAT. 9

IT MAY BE A RED FLAG
WHEN YOUR PARENT'S
ARE ARRESTED FOR CHILD
ABUSE BECAUSE THEY
PASSED ALL THEIR UGLY
GENES DOWN TO YOU.

# JULY 2011

## SUN. 10

IT MAY BE A RED FLAG WHEN
YOUR COMMUNION SUNDAY
ATTENDANCE TRIPLES AFTER
YOUR CHURCH SWITCHES
FROM GRAPE JUICE TO MAD
DOG 20/20.

# JULY 2011

## MON. 11

IT MAY BE A RED FLAG WHEN
A SEEING EYE DOG HAS A
SEEING EYE DOG.

# JULY 2011

## TUE. 12

IT MAY BE A READ FLAG
WHEN A DOG IS TREATED
FOR A STAPH INFECTION
FROM A MAN BITE.

# JULY 2011

## WED. 13

IT MAY BE A RED FLAG
WHEN YOU'VE ACQUIRED
ALL THE FINER THINGS
IN LIFE BUT FORGOT
WHERE YOU PUT THEM.

# JULY 2011

## THU. 14

IT MAY BE A RED FLAG
WHEN A HOBBIBLE SMELL
COMES FROM BENEATH
THE FLOOR UNDER YOUR
CHAIR AND EVERYBODY
LOOKS RIGHT AT YOU.

# JULY 2011

## FRI. 15

ITMAY BEA REDFLAGWHEN
THESPACEBAR
ONTHISKEYBOARDKEEPS
GETTINGSTUCK.

# JULY 2011

## SAT. 16

IT MAY BE A RED FLAG WHEN THE CURE FOR RACISM AS LISTED IN THE "BOOK OF UNNATURAL CURES THEY WANT YOU TO KNOW ABOUT" IS TO GO STOMPING AROUND IN A MINE FIELD.

# JULY 2011

## SUN. 17

IT MAY BE A RED FLAG WHEN
A CHURCH CHANGES ITS
NAME FROM "FAITH TEMPLE"
TO "FAITH TEMPORARY."

# JULY 2011

## MON. 18

IT MAY BE A RED FLAG WHEN YOUR DAD IS RESPECTED BY MOST EVERYBODY IN THE NEIGHBORHOOD EXCEPT YOU.

# JULY 2011

## TUE. 19

IT MAY BE A RED FLAG
WHEN YOU SEE A SIGN IN
A U.S. STORE THAT SAYS
"WE NO LONGER ACCEPT
AMERICAN CURRENCY."

## WED. 20

IT MAY BE A RED FLAG WHEN
YOUR BARBER WEARS REALLY
DARK GLASSES AND A DOG
BRINGS HIM HIS CLIPPERS.

# JULY 2011

## THU. 21

IT MAY BE A RED FLAG
WHEN IT WALKS AND
QUACKS LIKE A DUCK BUT
IT'S YOUR DOCTOR.

# JULY 2011

## FRI. 22

IT MAY BE A RED FLAG WHEN
A GIRL SAYS SHE'S SINGLE,
BUT WHEN SOME GUY WALKS
UP SHE YELLS "DUCK!"

# JULY 2011

## SAT. 23

IT MAY BE A RED FLAG WHEN
YOU BLEACH YOUR SKIN AND
STRAIGHTEN YOUR HAIR TO
LOOK LIKE THE VERY PEOPLE
YOU SAY YOU HATE.

# JULY 2011

## SUN. 24

IT MAY BE A RED FLAG WHEN
NOBODY CAN HEAR YOU OVER
THE DEAF MUTE SITTING
BESIDE YOU IN PRAISE AND
WORSHIP SERVICE.

# JULY 2011

## MON. 25

IT MAY BE A RED FLAG WHEN
YOUR PODIATRIST HAS TWO
WOODEN FEET.

# JULY 2011

## TUE. 26

IT MAY BE A RED FLAG
WHEN A BAR HAS A TWO
DRINK MINIMUM ON ALL
STRYCHNINE COCKTAILS.

# JULY 2011

## WED. 27

IT MAY BE A RED FLAG WHEN
THE HANDWRITING ON YOUR
PRESCRIPTION IS SO BAD
THAT THE PHARMACIST GAVE
YOU INSULTS INSTEAD
OF INSULIN.

# JULY 2011

## THU. 28

IT MAY BE A RED FLAG WHEN
YOU BUY PERFUME FOR YOUR
WIFE FROM A SHOP NAMED
"STANKY MAE'S."

# JULY 2011

## FRI. 29

IT MAY BE A RED FLAG
WHEN YOUR GRAND MA
DUMPS A PILE OF CHANGE
AT THE REGISTER TO PAY
FOR GROCERIES..............
OUT OF HER BRA.

# JULY 2011

## SAT. 30

IT MAY BE A RED FLAG WHEN
YOUR PILOT ANNOUNCES
THAT THERE WILL BE A FOUR
COCKTAIL TAKE OFF DELAY.

# JULY 2011

## SUN. 31

IT MAY BE A RED FLAG
WHEN A GUY CARRIES
A SIGN THAT SAYS,
**"GOD HATES FAGS"**
AND WONDERS WHY HE IS
ALWAYS GETTING BEAT UP.

# AUGUST 2011

## MON. 1

IT MAY BE A RED FLAG WHEN YOU GET ON THE BUS AND THE DRIVER ASK YOU FOR DIRECTIONS.

# AUGUST 2011

## TUE. 2

IT MAY BE A RED FLAG
WHEN "ICE T" REFUSES
FREE ACTING LESSONS.

# AUGUST 2011

## WED. 3

IT MAY BE A RED FLAG WHEN
YOU HAVE MISMANAGED
MONEY ALL YOUR LIFE AND
THINK THAT WINNING THE
LOTTERY WILL SOLVE ALL
YOUR PROBLEMS.

# AUGUST 2011

## THU. 4

IT MAY BE A RED FLAG WHEN
YOU PASSED A TEST ONLY
BECAUSE YOU COPIED OFF
FORREST GUMP.

# AUGUST 2011

## FRI. 5

IT MAY BE A RED FLAG WHEN
ALL THE ANTS IN YOUR ANT
FARM HAVE RELOCATED.

# AUGUST 2011

## SAT. 6

IT MAY BE A RED FLAG WHEN,
NO ONE TOLD YOU THAT YOU
ARE ON THE MAIDEN VOYAGE
OF A REMOTE CONTROL
PASSENGER JET.

# AUGUST 2011

## SUN. 7

IT MAY BE A RED FLAG
WHEN YOU RUN A HOMELESS
PERSON OVER ON YOUR WAY
TO EAT AFTER CHURCH.

# AUGUST 2011

## MON. 8

IT MAY BE A RED FLAG WHEN
PEOPLE HAVE TO CLEAN THEIR
FEET AFTER THEY LEAVE
YOUR HOUSE.

# AUGUST 2011

## TUE. 9

IT MAY BE A RED FLAG
WHEN THE DRIVE TEST
EXAMINER OFFERS YOU A
HIT OFF HIS CRACK PIPE
TO SETTLE YOUR NERVES.

# AUGUST 2011

## WED. 10

IT MAY BE A RED FLAG
WHEN ON THE DOOR OF A
CRACK HOUSE IS WRITTEN
"ALL YOU CAN SMOKE
JUST TIL YOU BROKE."

# AUGUST 2011

## THU. 11

IT MAY BE A RED FLAG
WHEN GOD WAS HANDING
OUT BRAINS YOU THOUGHT
HE SAID PLANES AND SAID
"FORGET IT, I DON'T FLY."

# AUGUST 2011

## FRI. 12

IT MAY BE A RED FLAG
WHEN AN ARMLESS JOCKEY
PULLS ALONG SIDE YOU
IN A RACE AND ASKS YOU
TO WHIP HIS HORSE.

# AUGUST 2011

## SAT. 13

IT MAY BE A RED FLAG WHEN
YOU CALL THE SUICIDE
HOTLINE AND A RECORDING
OF A PRIEST GIVES YOU YOUR
LAST RITES AND HANGS UP.

# AUGUST 2011

## SUN. 14

IT MAY BE A RED FLAG WHEN
THE NAME OF YOUR CHURCH
HAS CHANGED FROM "MT.
OLIVE" TO "MT.MARTINI."

# AUGUST 2011

## MON. 15

IT MAY BE A RED FLAG
WHEN YOU START THE FIRST
CHAPTER OF A.A.S.D.
"ALCOHOLICS AGAINST SOBER
DRIVING."

# AUGUST 2011

## TUE. 16

IT MAY BE A RED FLAG WHEN
YOUR DOCTOR ASK,"WHAT
DO YOU WANT ON YOUR
TOMBSTONE?"

# AUGUST 2011

## WED. 17

IT MAY BE A RED FLAG
WHEN YOUR COUSIN THE
"CLEPTO" ASK YOU TO TAKE
HER TO THE STORE TO
PICK UP A FEW THINGS.

# AUGUST 2011

## THU. 18

IT MAY BE A RED FLAG WHEN
A DOG ACTUALLY SAYS
"BOW WOW"
WHEN IT BARKS.

# AUGUST 2011

## FRI. 19

IT MAY BE A RED FLAG WHEN
YOUR FEET ARE SO BIG THAT
THEY ARRIVE FIVE MINUTES
AHEAD OF YOU.

# AUGUST 2011

## SAT. 20

IT MAY BE A RED FLAG
WHEN A MOTIVATIONAL
SPEAKER BREAKS DOWN
AND STARTS BALLING.

# AUGUST 2011

## SUN. 21

IT MAY BE A RED FLAG
WHEN YOU ARE KICKED OUT
OF THE COUNTRY CLUB FOR
WETTING IN THE POOL;

FROM THE HIGH DIVING BOARD.

# AUGUST 2011

## MON. 22

IT MAY BE A RED FLAG
WHEN YOUR PSYCHIATRIST
ASKS TO BORROW SOME
OF YOUR MEDICATION.

# AUGUST 2011

## TUE. 23

IT MAY BE A RED FLAG WHEN
THE CAVEMAN GETS A TICKET
FOR NO INSURANCE.

# AUGUST 2011

## WED. 24

IT MAY BE A RED FLAG
WHEN YOUR WIFE SLEEPS
SO BAD, THAT SHE'S
BEEN COURT ORDERED
TO ATTEND DOMESTIC
VIOLENCE CLASSES.

# AUGUST 2011

## THU. 25

IT MAY BE A RED FLAG
WHEN A POLICEMAN'S
UNIFORM IS MADE UP
FROM THREE DIFFERENT
MILITARY BRANCHES.

# AUGUST 2011

## FRI. 26

IT MAY BE A RED FLAG WHEN
YOUR GRAND PA MOWS HIS
YARD THAT HAS NO GRASS
WITH HIS LAWNMOWER
THAT HAS NO BLADE.

# AUGUST 2011

## SAT. 27

IT MAY BE A RED FLAG WHEN
THE ELEPHANT MAN SAYS HE
CAN'T TRAVEL BECAUSE HE
HAS NO TRUNK.

# AUGUST 2011

## SUN. 28

IT MAY BE A RED FLAG WHEN
YOU WAKE UP TO THE SOUND
OF A LARGE DOG GROWLING
IN YOUR BEDROOM, BUT YOU
DON'T HAVE ONE.

# AUGUST 2011

## MON. 29

IT MAY BE A RED FLAG
WHEN YOU HAVE SO MANY
EXCUSES THAT THEY KEEP
COMING 20 MINUTES
AFTER YOU HAVE GONE.

# AUGUST 2011

## TUE. 30

IT MAY BE A RED FLAG WHEN THERE'S AN ELEPHANT IN YOUR TRUNK WITHOUT ONE.

# AUGUST 2011

## WED. 31

IT MAY BE A RED FLAG WHEN
THE NEW SHELLFISH PLATTER
ON THE MENU IS CHICKEN
BEAKS STUFFED WITH TUNA.

# SEPTEMBER 2011

# THU. 1

IT MAY BE A RED FLAG WHEN YOUR WIFE'S DOMESTIC VIOLENCE COUNSELOR TELLS HER TO BRING IN HER DOORKNOBS FOR THERAPY.

# SEPTEMBER 2011

## FRI. 2

IT MAY BE A RED FLAG
WHEN YOUR WIFE CHANGES
FROM " FULL OF LOVE
LULU" TO "RUNNING OVER
WITH HATE HANNA."

# SEPTEMBER 2011

## SAT. 3

IT MAY BE A RED FLAG WHEN
A PEEPING TOM SAYS
"NO THANKS I'M JUST
LOOKING."

# SEPTEMBER 2011

## SUN. 4

IT MAY BE A RED FLAG WHEN
YOU KEEP LUSTING AND AIN'T
GOT BUT ONE EYE LEFT.

# SEPTEMBER 2011

## MON. 5

IT MAY BE A RED FLAG
WHEN YOU KEEP ON
KISSING THE PRINCE TO
GET THE FROG BACK.

# SEPTEMBER 2011

## TUE. 6

IT MAY BE A RED FLAG WHEN
OSAMA BIN LADEN SENDS
OUT INVITATIONS TO A
FALLOUT SHELTER PARTY.

# SEPTEMBER 2011

## WED. 7

IT MAY BE A RED FLAG WHEN
IT MAKES ME HAPPY WHEN
SOMEBODY DOES SOMETHING
STUPID SO I CAN PUT IT IN
THIS RED FLAG A DAY BOOK.

# SEPTEMBER 2011

## THU. 8

IT MAY BE A RED FLAG WHEN
A PERSON ACTUALLY SAYS
"BOO HOO"
WHEN THEY CRY.

# SEPTEMBER 2011

## FRI. 9

IT MAY BE A RED FLAG WHEN YOU CALL 411 AND THE OPERATOR PUMPS YOU FOR INFORMATION.

# SEPTEMBER 2011

## SAT. 10

IT MAY BE A RED FLAG
WHEN YOUR FEET STINK SO
BAD THAT YOUR SOX AND
SHOES RAN AWAY WITH
YOUR WIFE AND KIDS.

# SEPTEMBER 2011

## SUN. 11

IT MAY BE A RED FLAG WHEN
YOUR PASTOR WON'T LEAVE
HIS HOUSE UNTIL HIS
CONCEALED WEAPONS PERMIT
IS RENEWED.

# SEPTEMBER 2011

## MON. 12

IT MAY BE A RED FLAG
WHEN AN "ALL YOU CAN EAT
BUFFET" HAS YOUR FAMILY
PORTRAIT ON THE WALL
WITH A SLASH THROUGH IT.

# SEPTEMBER 2011

## TUE. 13

IT MAY BE A RED FLAG WHEN
YOUR CELL PHONE QUITS
EVERY TIME THE STRING
BREAKS ON THE
TIN CAN.

# SEPTEMBER 2011

## WED. 14

IT MAY BE A RED FLAG
WHEN YOUR DENTIST HAS
ONLY THREE TEETH AND
TWO OF THEM ARE IN
HIS POCKET.

# SEPTEMBER 2011

## THU. 15

IT MAY BE A RED FLAG WHEN
YOU SEE AN ABANDONED
YELLOW RYDER TRUCK PARKED
ON THE WHITE HOUSE LAWN.

# SEPTEMBER 2011

## FRI. 16

IT MAY BE A RED FLAG
WHEN A NIGHT DRIVER ON A
NITROGLYCERINE TRUCK
HAS NARCOLEPSY.

# SEPTEMBER 2011

## SAT. 17

IT MAY BE A RED FLAG WHEN YOU HEAR LOUD MUSIC AND CLINKING GLASSES COMING FROM THE COCKPIT OF AN IN FLIGHT JETLINER.

# SEPTEMBER 2011

## SUN. 18

IT MAY BE A RED FLAG WHEN
YOU FALL ASLEEP IN CHURCH
AND WAKE UP CHAINED TO A
POST IN THE BASEMENT.

# SEPTEMBER 2011

## MON. 19

IT MAY BE A RED FLAG
WHEN "BUST A CAP"
BULLET REMOVAL KITS
ARE SOLD IN GHETTO
CONVENIENCE STORES.

# SEPTEMBER 2011

## TUE. 20

IT MAY BE A RED FLAG WHEN
A POLICEMAN IS ALL PUMPED
ABOUT HIS PROMOTION
TO THE MOUNTED PATROL
DIVISION UNTIL HE SEES
THE STICKHORSE.

# SEPTEMBER 2011

## WED. 21

IT MAY BE A RED FLAG WHEN OUR ARMY IS PROUD OF A SOLDIER WHEN HE HITS A TARGET 2 OUT OF 200 TIMES.

# SEPTEMBER 2011

# THU. 22

IT MAY BE A RED FLAG WHEN
A POLICE CAPTAIN THINKS
THAT S.W.A.T STANDS FOR
"SIPPING WINE AT TINA'S."

# SEPTEMBER 2011

## FRI. 23

IT MAY BE A RED FLAG
WHEN RAISEN BRAN
GOES FROM TWO SCOOPS
TO TWO RAISENS.

# SEPTEMBER 2011

## SAT. 24

IT MAY BE A RED FLAG
WHEN YOUR BOMB
DISPOSAL INSTRUCTOR
IS A RECORDING.

# SEPTEMBER 2011

## SUN. 25

IT MAY BE A RED FLAG
WHEN YOUR PASTOR'S
CLOTHES HAVE BEEN OUT
OF STYLE SO LONG THAT
THE CHAIN ON HIS ZOOT
SUIT IS RUSTED IN TWO.

# SEPTEMBER 2011

## MON. 26

IT MAY BE A RED FLAG WHEN
GOD WAS HANDING OUT
KNOWLEDGE YOU SAID,
"I DON'T THINK,"
.................... SOOOOO.

# SEPTEMBER 2011

## TUE. 27

IT MAY BE A RED FLAG WHEN
THE BIBLE SAYS THAT GOD
HAS THE VERY HAIRS OF
YOUR HEAD NUMBERED, BUT
ONLY NEEDS ONE HAND.

# SEPTEMBER 2011

## WED. 28

IT MAY BE A RED FLAG WHEN
YOU SNORE SO LOUD THAT
THE PEOPLE AT THE MONSTER
TRUCK RALLEY DOWN THE
STREET COMPLAIN.

# SEPTEMBER 2011

## THU. 29

IT MAY BE A RED FLAG WHEN
YOUR FIANCE'S ARREST
RECORD IS OLDER THAN YOU.

# SEPTEMBER 2011

## FRI. 30

IT MAY BE A RED FLAG WHEN
YOU BEEN WAITING ON THE
LORD SO LONG YOU FORGOT
WHAT FOR.

# OCTOBER 2011

## SAT. 1

IT MAY BE A RED FLAG
WHEN YOUR TV IS SO
OLD THAT WHEN YOUR
KIDS AIN'T HOME YOUR
REMOTE AIN'T EITHER.

www.redflagjoke.com

# OCTOBER 2011

## SUN. 2

IT MAY BE A RED FLAG WHEN
YOU DO SOMETHING SO
STUPID THAT IT ALMOST
SURPRISES GOD.

# OCTOBER 2011

## MON. 3

IT MAY BE A RED FLAG
WHEN YOUR REAL ESTATE
BROKER HAS BEEN EVICTED
FROM THE PROJECTS.

# OCTOBER 2011

## TUE. 4

IT MAY BE A RED FLAG WHEN
YOU FALL ASLEEP WATCHING
A CLIFF HANGER AND WAKE
UP TIED TO A TRAIN TRACK.

# OCTOBER 2011

## WED. 5

IT MAY BE A RED FLAG
WHEN THE WATER IN A
RESTAURANT IS SO BROWN
THAT IT DOUBLES
AS TEA.

# OCTOBER 2011

## THU. 6

IT MAY BE A RED FLAG WHEN YOUR PSYCHIATRIST MAKES AN APPOINTMENT FOR YOU WITH HIS PSYCHIATRIST'S PSYCHIATRIST.

# OCTOBER 2011

## FRI. 7

IT MAY BE A RED FLAG WHEN
YOUR FORTUNE COOKIE TELLS
YOU THAT YOUR WIFE'S
LOVER IS CHEATING ON HER.

# OCTOBER 2011

## SAT. 8

IT MAY BE A RED FLAG WHEN
WISDOM HAS THUS FAR
FAILED TO INHABIT YOUR
EXISTENCE.

# OCTOBER 2011

## SUN. 9

IT MAY BE A RED FLAG WHEN
A PASTOR SPENDS MORE TIME
MUD SLINGING
THAN GOD
SINGING.

# OCTOBER 2011

## MON. 10

IT MAY BE A RED FLAG WHEN
OLD PEOPLE ARE YOUNGER
THAN YOUR DAUGHTER'S
BOYFRIEND.

# OCTOBER 2011

## TUE. 11

IT MAY BE A RED FLAG WHEN
THE ELEPHANT MAN LOOKS
RATHER HANDSOME WHEN
STANDING BESIDE YOU.

# OCTOBER 2011

## WED. 12

IT MAY BE A RED FLAG WHEN
YOU DON'T KNOW THAT YOU
ARE NOT MEAN BECAUSE
YOU'RE SICK; YOU ARE SICK
BECAUSE YOU'RE MEAN.

# OCTOBER 2011

## THU. 13

IT MAY BE A RED FLAG WHEN
THE GOVERNOR CALLS FIVE
MINUTES BEFORE YOUR
EXECUTION BUT HIS WATCH
IS SIX MINUTES SLOW.

# OCTOBER 2011

## FRI. 14

IT MAY BE A RED FLAG WHEN
YOUR WIFE HAS A POST
DATED DEATH CERTIFICATE
WITH GUESS WHOSE NAME
ON IT.

# OCTOBER 2011

## SAT.15

IT MAY BE A RED FLAG WHEN
THE SUDDEN APPEARANCE
OF FRESH MEAT AT A
HOMELESS SHELTER IS
PROPORTIONANT TO THE
SUDDEN DISAPPEARANCE OF
SOME OF THE RESIDENTS.

# OCTOBER 2011

## SUN. 16

IT MAY BE A RED FLAG
WHEN A PERSON PROFESSES
VICTORY IN JESUS AND IS
ALWAYS COMPLAINING.

# OCTOBER 2011

## MON. 17

IT MAY BE A RED FLAG
WHEN THE ONLY THING
YOUR CHURCH'S BUILDING
FUND HAS PRODUCED IS
A BUNCH OF HATE FOR
BUILDING FUNDS.

## TUE. 18

IT MAY BE A RED FLAG WHEN
YOU WAKE UP TO THE SOUND
OF SOMEBODY WASHING
YOUR DISHES AT 3 AM BUT
YOU LIVE ALONE.

# OCTOBER 2011

## WED. 19

IT MAY BE A RED FLAG WHEN
FELLOW POLICE OFFICERS
HAVE A POOL ON WHEN
YOU'LL SHOOT SOMEBODY
ELSE AND HOW
MANY TIMES.

# OCTOBER 2011

## THU. 20

IT MAY BE A RED FLAG WHEN
YOUR HEAD MAKES YOUR HAT
LOOK LIKE A THIMBLE ON A
BROOMSTICK.

# OCTOBER 2011

## FRI. 21

IT MAY BE A RED FLAG WHEN YOU BOOK A VACATION AT DANNY DEMISE'S GRAVESIDE HOSPICE CASINO AND RESORT WITH EXCITING ACTIVITIES SUCH AS EYE BALL ROLLING, SPEED DEPENDS CHANGING, ENDURANCE DROOLING, AND INTERCOM YELLING.

# OCTOBER 2011

## SAT. 22

IT MAY BE A RED FLAG WHEN
SCHOOL ON SATURDAY,
YOU, AND WWE WRASSLING
HAVE ONE THING IN
COMMON; "NO CLASS."

# OCTOBER 2011

## SUN. 23

IT MAY BE A RED FLAG
WHEN YOUR GOALS ARE
SO LOW THAT THEY DON'T
REQUIRE SUPER NATURAL
INTERVENTION.

# OCTOBER 2011

## MON. 24

IT MAY BE A RED FLAG WHEN
YOU THINK THE OPPOSITE OF
PORNO IS PORYES.

# OCTOBER 2011

## TUE. 25

IT MAY BE A RED FLAG
WHEN YOUR DRIVER'S ED
TEACHER IS THE REIGNING
DEMOLITION DERBY KING.

# OCTOBER 2011

## WED. 26

IT MAY BE A RED FLAG
WHEN YOU LIST "SEXUAL
HARASSMENT" AS A HOBBY
ON A JOB APPLICATION.

# OCTOBER 2011

# THU. 27

IT MAY BE A RED FLAG
WHEN YOU WEAR A ROLEX
AND WORK FOR BILLY
BOB'S SHOE SHINE AND
CHITTLIN EMPORIUM.

# OCTOBER 2011

## FRI. 28

IT MAY BE A RED FLAG
WHEN A DOCTOR SAYS
IF YOU DON'T HAVE A
DISEASE, HE'LL GLADLY
HELP YOU CHOOSE ONE.

# OCTOBER 2011

## SAT. 29

IT MAY BE A RED FLAG
WHEN YOUR STUDENTS'
ONLY MEMORY OF YOU
IS THE SMELL OF VODKA
ON YOUR BREATH.

# OCTOBER 2011

## SUN. 30

IT MAY BE A RED FLAG WHEN
THE PASTOR HAS MOVED
YOUR SUNDAY SCHOOL
CLASS TO ANOTHER ROOM,
IN ANOTHER CHURCH,
IN ANOTHER TOWN, IN
ANOTHER STATE, IN
ANOTHER COUNTRY, ON
ANOTHER PLANET, IN
ANOTHER UNIVERSE.

# OCTOBER 2011

## MON. 31

IT MAY BE A RED FLAG
WHEN EVERYBODY STARTS
RUNNING AND SCREAMING
AFTER YOU TAKE OFF YOUR
HALLOWEEN MASK.

# NOVEMBER 2011

## TUE. 1

IT MAY BE A RED FLAG WHEN
AN OWL SAYS "WHAT?"

www.redflagjoke.com

# NOVEMBER 2011

## WED. 2

IT MAY BE A RED FLAG
WHEN A SKUNK HAS A
"FEBREZE" ADDICTION.

# NOVEMBER 2011

## THU. 3

IT MAY BE A RED FLAG WHEN
YOU BUY A CHEAP PAIR OF
ORTHOPEDIC SHOES CALLED
"DR. SHONUF STILL HURT."

# NOVEMBER 2011

## FRI. 4

IT MAY BE A RED FLAG
WHEN YOUR STEAK
FINGER SANDWICH IS
COMPLETE WITH BONES,
KNUCKLES AND NAILS.

# NOVEMBER 2011

## SAT. 5

IT MAY BE A RED FLAG
WHEN YOUR LAWYER'S
BREIFCASE HAS PLASTIC
HANDLES AND WAL MART
STAMPED ON THE SIDE.

# NOVEMBER 2011

## SUN. 6

IT MAY BE A RED FLAG WHEN
GOD CALLS YOU HOME CAUSE
YOU'RE JUST IN THE WAY
DOWN HERE.

# NOVEMBER 2011

## MON. 7

IT MAY BE A RED
FLAG WHEN YOU HEAR
SUBLIMITAL MESSAGES
COMING FROM A VIDEO OF
BARNEY AND FRIENDS.

# NOVEMBER 2011

## TUE. 8

IT MAY BE A RED FLAG
WHEN A CRATE FULL OF
RATTLESNAKES BOUNCES
OFF THE BACK OF YOUR
TRUCK AND BURSTS
IN YOUR MOTHER-IN-
LAW'S FRONT YARD.

# NOVEMBER 2011

## WED. 9

IT MAY BE A RED FLAG WHEN
YOU GO DEER HUNTING IN A
DEER SUIT.

# NOVEMBER 2011

## THU. 10

IT MAY BE A RED FLAG
WHEN THE CAMPGROUND
OWNER SAYS THERE ARE
NO PIT BULLS ALLOWED
AFTER HE MEETS YOUR
MOTHER-IN-LAW.

# NOVEMBER 2011

## FRI. 11

IT MAY BE A RED FLAG
WHEN HUNGRY PEOPLE ARE
REQUIRED TO HAVE ID,
PROOF OF INCOME AND
PROOF OF RESIDENCE TO
QUALIFY FOR FREE FOOD.

# NOVEMBER 2011

## SAT. 12

IT MAY BE A RED FLAG
WHEN YOU DON'T THINK
YOUR VISITING IN-LAWS
WILL MIND SLEEPING
IN THE GARAGE IN THE
DEAD OF WINTER WITH
NO HEAT OR BLANKETS.

# NOVEMBER 2011

## SUN. 13

IT MAY BE A RED FLAG
WHEN YOU HAVE HAD SO
MUCH PLASTIC SURGERY,
THAT JESUS DOESN'T
RECOGNIZE YOU AND SENDS
YOU AWAY......................
DOWN SOUTH.

# NOVEMBER 2011

## MON. 14

IT MAY BE A RED FLAG
WHEN YOUR DEPARTURE
IS HIGHLY FAVORED
OVER YOUR ARRIVAL.

# NOVEMBER 2011

## TUE. 15

IT MAY BE A RED FLAG WHEN
YOUR NOSE HAIRS ARE SO
LONG THAT YOU PULL THEM
OUT BY STEPPING ON THEM.

# NOVEMBER 2011

## WED. 16

IT MAY BEE AH RHED
PHLAGG WHIN EYE THENK
THET THUH SPEL SCHECK
ON THES KOMPUTER IS
RONG AN UM RITE.

# NOVEMBER 2011

## THU. 17

IT MAY BE A RED FLAG WHEN
THE SIGN IN FRONT OF YOUR
PODIATRIST'S OFFICE SAYS
"FOOT PARKING ONLY"
"ALL OTHERS WILL BE TOED."

# NOVEMBER 2011

## FRI. 18

IT MAY BE A RED FLAG
WHEN YOUR SISTER
MOVES OUT FROM HER
BOYFRIEND................AND
IN WITH HIS WIFE.

# NOVEMBER 2011

## SAT. 19

IT MAY BE A RED FLAG WHEN
THE CRACKHEADS NEXT DOOR
STOLE THE HORNS OFF YOUR
BILLY GOAT.

# NOVEMBER 2011

## SUN. 20

IT MAY BE A RED FLAG
WHEN THE PASTOR'S
WIFE IS ON HOUSE
ARREST FOR MOONING,
MORMONS, MUSLIMS,
METHODISTS, BAPTIST,
BUDDHISTS, CATHOLICS,
LUTHERANS,JEHOVA'S
WITNESSES, AND SEVEN
DAY ADVENTISTS.

# NOVEMBER 2011

# MON. 21

IT MAY BE A RED FLAG
WHEN YOU SEE A HANDICAP
PARKING SIGN ON A
PASSENGER JET DOCK.

# NOVEMBER 2011

## TUE. 22

IT MAY BE A RED FLAG
WHEN THE USHER PASSES
OUT EAR PLUGS AT YOUR
KID'S MUSIC RECITAL.

# NOVEMBER 2011

## WED. 23

IT MAY BE A RED FLAG
WHEN ALL THE HOUSES IN
YOUR NEIGHBORHOOD HAVE
BURGLAR BARS EXCEPT YOURS.

# NOVEMBER 2011

## THU. 24

IT MAY BE A RED FLAG
WHEN YOU LOOK UP STUPID
IN THE DICTIONARY
AND FIND SEVERAL U.S.
PRESIDENT'S PORTRAITS.

# NOVEMBER 2011

## FRI. 25

IT MAY BE A RED FLAG WHEN
YOUR DATE BRINGS HER OWN
UTENSILS TO DINNER THAT
APPEAR TO BE TWICE THE
NORMAL SIZE.

## SAT. 26

IT MAY BE A RED FLAG WHEN
YOU SEE A GUY USING ALL
HIS ENERGY TO REMAIN
UPRIGHT WHILE WALKING
INTO THE WIND, GO
OUTSIDE AND THERE ISN'T
EVEN A BREEZE.

# NOVEMBER 2011

## SUN. 27

IT MAY BE A RED FLAG WHEN
YOUR CHURCH SERVICE IS
CHANGED FROM TWO HOURS
LONG, TO FOUR SERVICES OF
THIRTY MINUTES EACH.

# NOVEMBER 2011

## MON. 28

IT MAY BE A RED FLAG WHEN
YOU ARE STANDING ON A
PLASTIC COVERED TRAPDOOR
DURING YOUR INTERVIEW
FOR A JOB WITH
THE MAFIA.

# NOVEMBER 2011

## TUE. 29

IT MAY BE A RED FLAG WHEN
MR. RODGERS IS SUCCEEDED
BY PEE WEE HERMAN.

# NOVEMBER 2011

## WED. 30

IT MAY BE A RED FLAG WHEN
MY HOME BOY THINKS THAT
THE RELENTLESS TRAILS OF
TERMITES ON HIS ROOF ARE
SUGAR ANTS.

# DECEMBER 2011

## THU. 1

IT MAY BE A RED FLAG WHEN
THE LADY IN THE GROCERY
STORE IS WINKING AND
SHAKING HER HEAD NO,
WHILE DEMONSTRATING
HER PRODUCT.

# DECEMBER 2011

## FRI. 2

IT MAY BE A RED FLAG WHEN
YOU THINK A FOOD COURT
IS WHERE IT IS DECIDED
IF BEANS ARE GUILTY OF
GIVING YOU GAS.

# SAT. 3

IT MAY BE A RED FLAG WHEN
YOU HEAR A SIGH OF RELIEF
FROM YOUR CAR EVERY TIME
YOU GET OUT.

# DECEMBER 2011

# SUN. 4

IT MAY BE A RED FLAG
WHEN YOUR CHURCH
MARQUEE SAYS,
"CARNAL CONSTRUCTION"
"FLESH AT WORK "

# DECEMBER 2011

## MON. 5

IT MAY BE A RED FLAG
WHEN YOUR "BEFORE" AND
"AFTER" PICTURES LOOK
LIKE THEY HAVE BEEN
SWITCHED.

# DECEMBER 2011

## TUE. 6

IT MAY BE A RED FLAG WHEN
A MAN TRYS TO CHANGE
A TIRE WHILE THE CAR IS
STILL MOVING.

# DECEMBER 2011

## WED. 7

IT MAY BE A RED FLAG WHEN
YOUR DOCTOR ALLOWS A
GROUP OF THIRD GRADERS ON
A FIELD TRIP TO VIEW YOUR
HEMOROID OPERATION.

# DECEMBER 2011

# THU. 8

IT MAY BE A RED FLAG WHEN
THEY CHANGE THE NATIONAL
BIRD FROM THE "BALD EAGLE"
TO THE "DOUGH DOUGH."

# DECEMBER 2011

## FRI. 9

IT MAY BE A RED FLAG
WHEN YOUR SON IS STILL
WEARING PAMPERS ON
HIS WEDDING DAY.

# DECEMBER 2011

## SAT. 10

IT MAY BE A RED FLAG WHEN
YOU THINK YOU'RE NOT AN
ALCOHOLIC BECAUSE YOU
ONLY DRINK BEER; ALL DAY
EVERY DAY.

# DECEMBER 2011

## SUN. 11

IT MAY BE A RED FLAG
WHEN YOU ARE A FISHER
OF MEN BUT STILL WON'T
GO FOR THE ONES ON
THE BOTTOM.

# DECEMBER 2011

## MON. 12

IT MAY BE A RED FLAG WHEN
YOU ARE SO OLD THAT YOU
BANKRUPTED THE LOTTERY
THAT AWARDED YOU A
DOLLAR A WEEK
FOR LIFE.

# DECEMBER 2011

## TUE. 13

IT MAY BE A RED FLAG WHEN
YOU HAVE ENOUGH CASH TO
BURN UP A WET ELEPHANT,
AND DO.

# DECEMBER 2011

## WED. 14

IT MAY BE A RED FLAG WHEN
YOUR CAR IS SO OLD, IT HAS
NO FLOORBOARDS AND IS
FOOT POWERED.

# DECEMBER 2011

## THU. 15

IT MAY BE A RED FLAG
WHEN YOU SPEND THIRTY
MINUTES REVIEWING THE
MENU WITH THE RONALD
MCDONALD STATUE.

# DECEMBER 2011

## FRI. 16

IT MAY BE A RED FLAG WHEN
AFTER BEING LATE SO MANY
TIMES FOR WORK, THAT ON
ARRIVAL YOU JUST NOD AND
YOUR BOSS SAYS "UH HUH."

# DECEMBER 2011

## SAT. 17

IT MAY BE A RED FLAG WHEN
YOUR PSYCHIATRIST LAYS ON
THE COUCH AND HANDS YOU
THE PAD AND PENCIL .

# DECEMBER 2011

## SUN. 18

IT MAY BE A BIG RED FLAG
WHEN YOU REFER TO "THE
LORD GOD," THE CREATOR OF
HEAVEN AND EARTH AS
"THE MAN UPSTAIRS."

# DECEMBER 2011

# MON. 19

IT MAY BE A RED FLAG WHEN
YOUR CHILD'S ENGLISH
TEACHER CALLS TO DISCUSS
HIS FAILING GRADE AND
YOU CAN'T UNDERSTAND
A WORD SHE SAYS.

# DECEMBER 2011

## TUE. 20

IT MAY BE A RED FLAG WHEN
AN AIRPLANE'S INSTRUMENT
PANEL IS IN BRAILLE.

# DECEMBER 2011

## WED. 21

IT MAY BE A RED FLAG
WHEN YOU REFER TO
YOUR BELOVED BRIDE AND
FAITHFUL HELP MEET AS
"THE WIFE."

# DECEMBER 2011

## THU. 22

IT MAY BE A RED FLAG WHEN
YOUR BOSS'S I.Q. NUMBER
AND SHOE SIZE ARE THE
SAME SIZE .

# DECEMBER 2011

## FRI. 23

IT MAY BE A RED FLAG
WHEN YOU RECEIVE HATE
MAIL FROM CHRISTMAS
CAROLERS EVERY YEAR
ABOUT THIS TIME.

# DECEMBER 2011

## SAT. 24

IT MAY BE A RED FLAG WHEN YOU THINK AN ATTIC HAS A DRUG PROBLEM.

# DECEMBER 2011

## SUN. 25

IT MAY BE A RED FLAG
WHEN YOU ATTRIBUTE
MORE POWER TO A FAT
MAN IN A RED SUIT THAN
THE CREATOR OF WORLD.

# DECEMBER 2011

## MON. 26

IT MAY BE A RED FLAG WHEN
YOU GET THIRD PLACE IN A
BEAUTY CONTEST THAT WAS
WON BY AN ORANGUTAN.

# DECEMBER 2011

## TUE. 27

IT MAY BE A RED FLAG WHEN
SEE A KANGAROO WITH A
BACK POCKET.

## WED. 28

IT MAY BE A RED FLAG
WHEN JOE CAMEL GOES
IN FOR CHEMO.

# DECEMBER 2011

## THU. 29

IT MAY BE A RED FLAG WHEN
McGRUFF THE CRIME DOG
IS BUSTED FOR RECEIVING
STOLEN MERCHANDISE.

# DECEMBER 2011

## FRI. 30

IT MAY BE A RED FLAG WHEN
AN EXPIRATION DATE HAS
BEEN STAMPED OVER ON A
CARTON OF MILK.

## SAT. 31

IT MAY BE A RED FLAG
WHEN NOT ONE THESE 365
PROVERBIAL RED FLAGS FOR
LIFE AND LAUGHTER HAVE
MADE YOU LAUGH, MADE YOU
CRY, OR MOST IMPORTANTLY
## <u>MADE YOU THINK.</u>

# JANUARY 2012

## SUN. 1

IT IS DEFINITELY A RED FLAG
WHEN THERE ARE 365 MORE
PROVERBIAL RED FLAGS JUST
WAITING AND READY TO
STRIKE THIS YEAR.

## GOD BLESS YOU AND
## KEEP YOU ALL

BY DONALD J. PALMER SR. AUGUST 2010
AKA COLORADO BANNER
www.redflagjoke.com